This Book Belongs To:

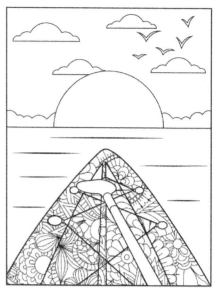

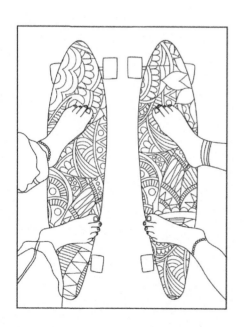

Thank you for your purchase!

We are a small, family run business and appreciate each and every order...

Want some FREE printable coloring pages?

For your FREE printable coloring pages, please join our mailing list at:

www.ellastevensondesigns.com

or

○ @ellastevensondesigns

Color Test Page

A quick tip:

The paper Amazon uses to print coloring books is best suited for colored pencils and gel pens. If using felt tip pens, we recommend putting a piece of card or paper behind the page you are coloring to prevent any bleed through.

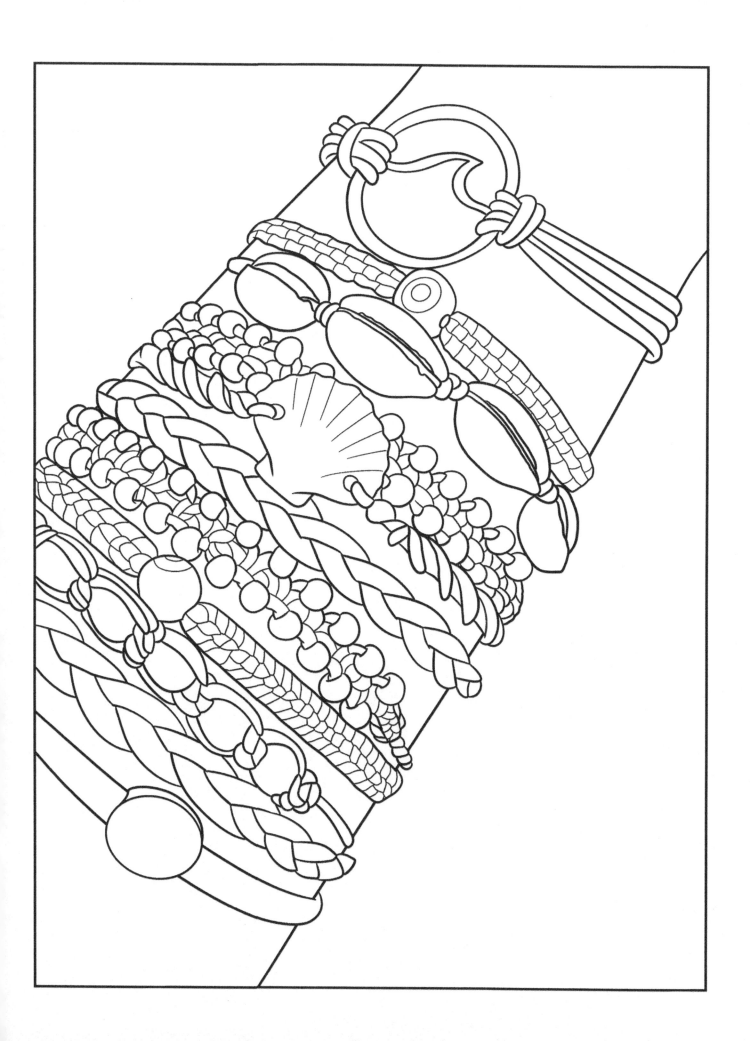

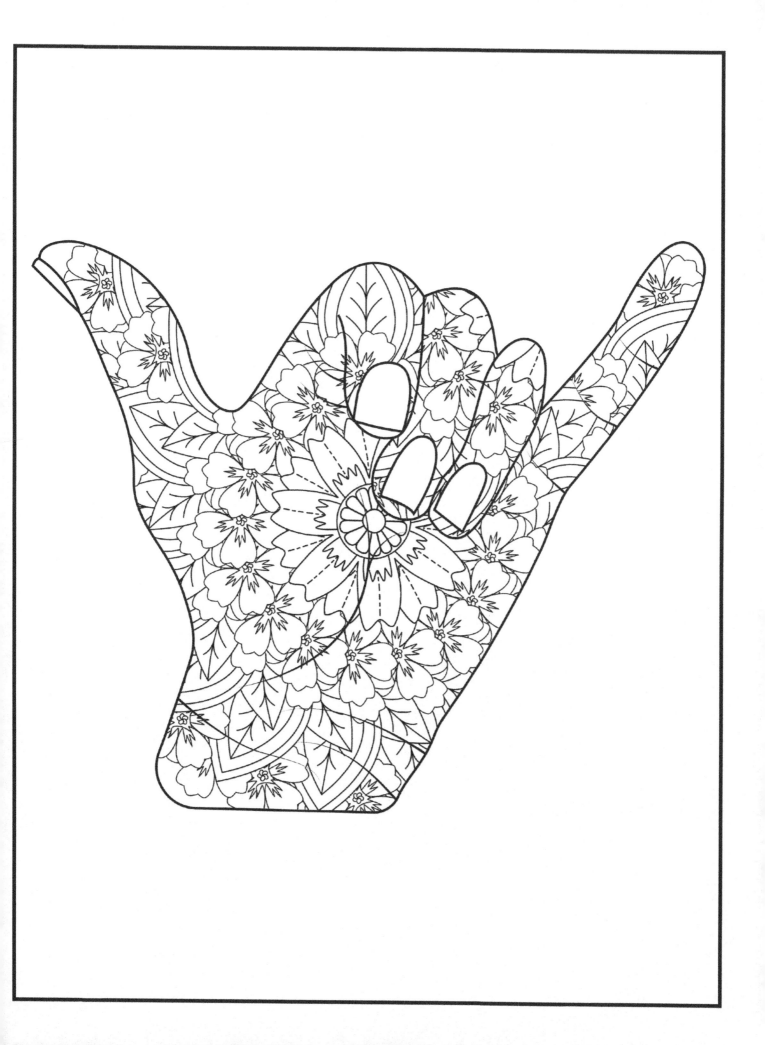

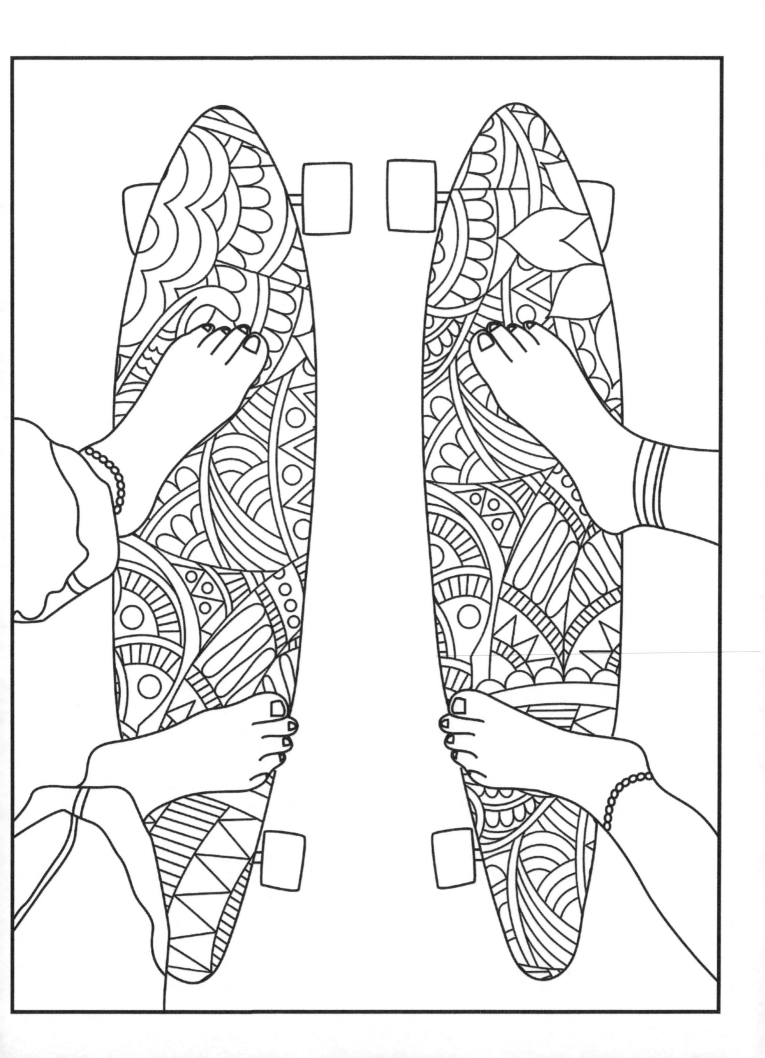

We hope you enjoyed the coloring book!

We would love you to leave a review on Amazon - it really helps other people who love coloring to find our books.

The easiest way to do this is to find the book on Amazon (Ella Stevenson Coloring Books), scroll to the customer review section and share your thoughts.

Thank you!

All available through Amazon:

Amazon.com
Amazon.co.uk
Amazon.ca
Amazon.com.au

Or visit the links on our website or Instagram Bio

www.ellastevensondesigns.com

 @ellastevensondesigns

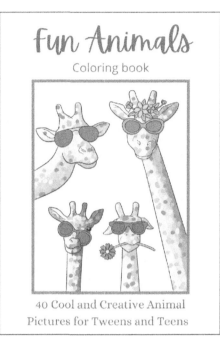

Fun Animals
Coloring book

40 Cool and Creative Animal
Pictures for Tweens and Teens

Fun Animals
Coloring Book

Book 2

40 Cool and Creative Animal Pictures
For Tweens and Teens

COLORING BOOK
For Teen Girls

40 Fun and Creative Designs

Kawaii
Coloring Book

50 Cute and Creative Designs
For Tween and Teen Girls

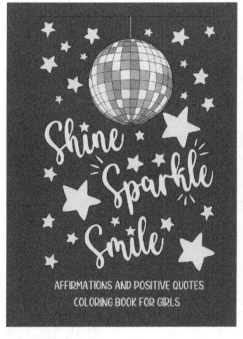

Shine Sparkle Smile

AFFIRMATIONS AND POSITIVE QUOTES
COLORING BOOK FOR GIRLS

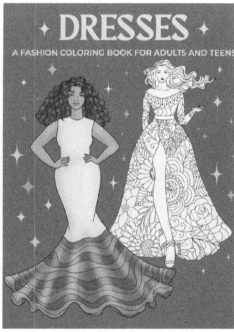

DRESSES
A FASHION COLORING BOOK FOR ADULTS AND TEENS

Made in the USA
Las Vegas, NV
25 November 2023

81488477R00050